Programming for Students with BASIC

Craig Whitmore

Published by Lulu.com
Bakersfield, CA

ISBN 978-1-105-36239-2

© 2011, Craig Whitmore

All Rights Reserved. Contact author at craigwhitmore@yahoo.com for reprinting permission regarding class sets.

First Edition

Table of Contents

Introduction to BASIC
   What is BASIC?... 1
   History of Use... 1
   Programming Languages........................... 2
   Text-Based Games..................................... 2
   ASCII Art.. 3

Tutorial Programs
Introduction
      Basic commands for BASIC............... 4
1 Printing
      Worksheet 1 – basic commands............6
      Program 1 – printing practice...............7
2 Inputting Variables
      Worksheet 2 – inputting variables..........8
      Program 2 – psychologist.....................9
3 Printing Variables
      Worksheet 3 – printing variables..........10
      Program 3 – madlibs..........................11
4 ASCII art
      ASCII art online............................ 12
      Worksheet 4 – creating ASCII art........ 13
      Program 4 – ASCII art in BASIC......... 14
5 Math Functions
      Worksheet 5 – basic math.................. 15
      Program 5 – calculator...................... 16
6 Looping
      Worksheet 6 – looping...................... 17
      Program 6 – liftoff......................... 18
7 Conditional Statements
      Worksheet 7 – conditional statements... 19
      Program 7 – riddle game....................20
8 Random Numbers
      Worksheet 8 – random numbers.......... 21
      Program 8 – number guessing.............22
9 Text Games Intro
      Zork online game...........................23
      Zork worksheet.............................24
10 CYOA Game
      CYOA adventure rules.....................25
      CYOA introduction worksheet............ 26
      CYOA flowchart worksheet............... 27
      CYOA flowchart planning................ 28
      CYOA programming code............... 29

Additional Worksheets
   CYOA Mini-Quiz.......................... 31
   CYOA Game Review....................... 32

Appendices
   Programming Tips and Tricks................ 34
   Advanced Text-Adventure Games.......... 35
   Description of Mr. Whitmore's Games
      Atlantis Adventure..................... 40
      Castle Adventure...................... 41
      Excelsior............................... 42
      Pirate Adventure...................... 43
      Spy Adventure........................ 44
   Answers for Teachers
      (Selected Worksheets)................. 44

What is BASIC?

BASIC (an acronym which stands for **Beginner's All-purpose Symbolic Instruction Code**) is a family of high-level programming languages designed to be easy to use.

The original Dartmouth BASIC was designed in 1964 at Dartmouth College in New Hampshire, USA to provide computer access to non-science students. At the time, nearly all use of computers required writing custom software, which was something only scientists and mathematicians tended to do. BASIC and its variants became widespread on microcomputers in the late 1970s and 1980s.

BASIC remains popular to this day in a handful of highly modified dialects and new languages such as Microsoft Visual Basic. In 2006, 59% of developers for the .NET platform used Visual Basic .NET as their only programming language.[1]

History of Use

The original BASIC language was designed in 1964 by **John Kemeny and Thomas Kurtz**[2] and implemented by a team of Dartmouth students under their direction. Being able to use a computer to support teaching and research was quite novel at the time. The eight design principles of BASIC were:

- Be easy for beginners to use.
- Be a general-purpose programming language.
- Allow advanced features to be added for experts (while keeping the language simple for beginners).
- Be interactive.
- Provide clear and friendly error messages.
- Respond quickly for small programs.
- Not to require an understanding of computer hardware.
- Shield the user from the operating system.

The designers of the language decided to make the compiler available free of charge so that the language would become widespread. They made it available to high schools in the Hanover area and put a considerable amount of effort into promoting the language.

In 1975, MITS released Altair BASIC, developed by **Bill Gates and Paul Allen** as the company Micro-Soft, which grew into today's corporate giant, Microsoft. As the popularity of BASIC spread, newer computer designs also introduced their own version of the language or had Micro-Soft port its version to their platform.

When three major new computers were introduced in 1977 (in what Byte Magazine would later call the "**1977 Trinity**"[3]) all three had BASIC as their primary programming language and operating environment. Commodore Business Machines, Apple II and TRS-80 all introduced similar versions of the language. Most of the home computers of the 1980s had a ROM-resident BASIC interpreter, allowing the machines to boot directly into BASIC. Because of this legacy, **there are more dialects of BASIC than there are of any other programming language**.

Programming Languages

A programming language is an artificial language designed to express computations that can be performed by a machine. There are many different programming languages. Some are tiny scripts written by individual hobbyists others are huge systems written by hundreds of programmers. Programs must balance speed, size, and simplicity on systems ranging from microcontrollers to supercomputers.

The first programming languages predate the modern computer and were the "programmable" looms of the 1800's. The first high-level programming language was **Plankalkül**, developed by Konrad Zuse in 1944 for the German Z3.

Early programmers used machine language programs or first generation language (1GL) which are primitive (and cumbersome) programming languages. Second generation languages (2GL) are known as assembly languages. In the 1950s, 2GL was followed by the development of "third generation" programming languages (3GL), which are more abstract and "portable".

The period from the 1960s to the late 1970s brought the development of the major language groups still in use, such as **Simula**, **Smalltalk**, **C**, and **Prolog**. The 1980s were years of relative consolidation, with **C++** and **Pascal**. The rapid growth of the Internet in the mid-1990s created opportunities for new languages. **Perl** became common in dynamic websites and **Java** came to be used for server-side programming. Markup languages like XML or HTML are not generally considered programming languages.

Today, there is no overarching classification scheme for programming languages. Languages commonly arise by combining the elements of several predecessor languages with new ideas. Ideas that originate in one language will leap suddenly across gaps to appear in an entirely different programming family. There are (or have been) over 8,500 different types of programming languages used throughout the world.[4]

Text-Based Games

A text game or text-based game is a video game that uses text characters instead of graphics. Text-based games, which are typically easier to write and require less processing power than graphical games, were common from 1970 to 1990, but are still used today. You can find people who still play MUDs (multi-user dungeon) and explore interactive fiction. Many beginning programmers still create these types of games to familiarize themselves with a programming language.

Here are a few of the popular early text games:

Oregon Trail   1971 by Don Rawitsch
Colossal Cave Adventure 1976 by Will Crowther
Zork   1977 by Tim Anderson, Marc Blank, Bruce Daniels and Dave Lebling
Rogue   1980 by Michael Toy, Glenn Wichman and Ken Arnold

ASCII Art

ASCII art (American Standard Code for Information Interchange) is a graphic design technique that uses computers for presentation and consists of pictures pieced together from the 95 printable characters defined by the ASCII Standard from 1963. The term is also loosely used to refer to text based art in general. ASCII art can be created with any text editor, and is often used with free-form languages. Most examples of ASCII art require a fixed-width font such as Courier to be viewed correctly.

Among the oldest known examples of ASCII art are the creations by computer-art pioneer Kenneth Knowlton from around 1966, who was working for Bell Labs at the time. "Studies in Perception I" by Ken Knowlton and Leon Harmon from 1966 shows some examples of their early ASCII art.[5]

One of the main reasons ASCII art was born was because early printers often lacked graphics ability. Examples of ASCII-style art predating the modern computer era can be found in the June 1939, July 1948 and October 1948 editions of Popular Mechanics.[6] ASCII art was also used in early e-mail when images could not be embedded. The ASCII art phenomenon continues to exist in the social and mobile web, even when constrained to only 140 unicode characters, as exhibited by Twitter channels such as @TW1TT3Rart .[7]

Different techniques can be used in ASCII art to obtain different artistic effects:

```
      Line art (creating shapes)      Solid art (creating filled shapes)      Shading (creating contrasts)
            .--.      /\                   .g@8g.   db                         :$#$:   "4b.  ':.
            '--'     /__\                  'Y8@P'  d88b                        :$#$:    "4b. ':.
```

The simplest forms of ASCII art are combinations of two or three characters for expressing emotion in text ('emoticons' or 'smileys') like this winking face: ;-) ASCII art has been used to create animations and even music videos.[8,9] Some programs (and web pages) allow one to automatically convert an image to ASCII art.[10]

---

1   "Trends 2006: Language and Platform Adoption", Forrester Research, Inc., March 2006.
2   Kurtz, Thomas E., History of Programming Languages, http://cis-alumni.org/TKurtz.html. Retrieved 2011-09-13.
3   "Most Important Companies". Byte Magazine. September 1995. Retrieved 2008-06-10.
4   "HOPL: an interactive Roster of Programming Languages". Australia: Murdoch University. Retrieved 2009-06-01.
5   Carlson, Wayne 2003 "1966 Studies in Perception I by Ken Knowlton and Leon Harmon (Bell Labs)"
6   Cumbrowski, Carsten (2007-02-14), "Keyboard Text Art From Over Twenty Years Before ASCII", http://roysac.com,   Retrieved 2008-03-05
7   "ASCII art in social and mobile web, as exhibited by @TwitterArt channel". http://twitter.com/#%21/TW1TT3Rart/   Retrieved 2011-06-01.
8   Jansen, Simon. 2011 "Star Wars Asciimation", http://asciimation.co.nz. Retrieved 2011-09-09.
9   Hansen, Beck, "Black Tambourine", http://www.youtube.com/watch?v=wEXaEYpifhg. Retrieved 2011-09-09.
10 "Picascii", http://picascii.com/. Retrieved 2011-0-09.

Collected and modified from Wikipedia.com ~ August, 2011

NAME_____

Basic Commands for BASIC (Macintosh)

```
        cls
print (?)
run (⌘-r)
    rem (')
        goto
            ;
              ,
          \\    //
                :
end (⌘-.)
list(⌘-l)
        new
```

NAME_____

Basic Commands for BASIC (Windows/Linux)

```
        cls
    print (?)
            run
    rem (')
        goto
            ;
              ,
          \\    //
                :
end (ctrl-c)
        list
            new
```

4

NAME _____

Basic Commands for BASIC (Macintosh)

cls	clears the screen
print (?)	displays text or variables
run (⌘-r)	executes the current program
rem (`)	remark, leaves a note, ignored by program
goto	jumps program to a line #
;	keeps next text on same line
,	tabs displayed text over
" "	enclose the text you want displayed
:	allows multiple commands on one line #
end (⌘-.)	stops program
list (⌘-l)	displays current program
new	erases current program

NAME _____

Basic Commands for BASIC (Windows/Linux)

cls	clears the screen
print (?)	displays text or variables
run	executes the current program
rem (`)	remark, leaves a note, ignored by program
goto	jumps program to a line #
;	keeps next text on same line
,	tabs displayed text over
" "	enclose the text you want displayed
:	allows multiple commands on one line #
end (ctrl-c)	stops program
list	displays current program
new	erases current program

© Craig Whitmore, 2011

Worksheet #1 - Basic Commands Practice

NAME _____

Part A
Type in the following commands, press <RETURN> and write what happens.

    cls

    print "hi"

    ? "how"

    print "are";

    print ,"you?"

Part B
Now type in this program. <u>Include the line numbers</u>. When you are finished, type "run" and press return.

```
10 cls
20 print "--type in your name here--"
30 goto 20
```

1. Line 30 puts your program into a never-ending loop. Which keys will stop it? _____
   (***WARNING*** In Linux, you can only use the stop keys once, then the program will freeze!)

After you run the first program, modify line 20 by retyping it and adding a semicolon at the end. Don't worry about putting it in the right order, the program will do that. Then run the program again.

```
20 print "--type in your name here--";
```
← Make sure to add the semicolon at the end this time!

2. What is different when it runs this time?

Save your program to your Documents Folder. Click on "File - Save" and call it "firstprogram.bas".
   (*** In Linux, type **save "Documents/firstprogram.bas"**)

3. What do you think the ".bas" suffix tells the computer?

© Craig Whitmore, 2011

PROGRAM #1 – PRINTING PRACTICE

Create a program to print out EXACTLY what is shown below: (Choose one of them) Use the tab command to space out the lines. You should have at least 5 lines in your program. If your teacher wants you to, save it as "program 1.bas".

Program A

```
See Tom and Mary.
        Tom and Mary are running.
                Run Tom.   Run Mary.

Tom and Mary like running.
```

You need to number your program like this:

```
10 print "See Tom …
20 print ,"Tom and …
……
```

Program B

```
I will not eat them with a mouse.
        I will not eat them in a house.
                I will not eat them here or there.
                I will not eat them anywhere.
        I do not eat green eggs and ham.
I do not like them, Sam-I-am.
```

Post-Program Questions

1. What does a comma tell Chipmunk Basic to do?

2. How can you get a print line that is blank?

3. Why do you think it's a good idea to number your program by 10's?

4. What is the short-cut command for 'print'?

5. Did your program work correctly the first time? If not, what did you have to fix?

WORKSHEET 2 - INPUTTING VARIABLES

NAME _____

Inputting is allowing the user to enter _____ that the program uses for calculations. It involves the use of _____. The variables can be one of two types:

Variable name	Data type	Sign or symbol	Examples

1. Type in and run the following program. What happens?
   ```
   10 input a
   20 print ,a
   ```
   What happens if you enter "hello" when you run the program?

   TEACHER'S INITIALS

2. Change and run these lines.
   ```
   10 input a$
   20 print ,a$
   ```
   How is the program different now?

3. What variable name would you give to each of the following? (hint: is it a number or a word?)

   A variable for …

   … your age in years   **age**   … your favorite type of soda   **soda$**

   … your favorite color _____   … how many pets you have _____

   … the name of a car _____   … two numbers to be added _____

   … a person's weight in pounds _____

4. Variables can be used by the program for _____. (caolnlacuits)

Type in and run this program. What does it do?
```
10 input a
20 input b
30 c = a + b
40
```
You create this line to print out the sum of a & b
(hint: it can be as small as 2 characters)

5. Change the program above to **multiply** the two variables instead of adding them.
   What would the new line 30 be?

PROGRAM #2 – PSYCHOLOGIST

```
10 rem program #2 - psychologist
20 cls
30                                            @@@@@@
40      Use lines 30-70 to draw an ASCII art  @-o-o-@
50      picture of the Psychologist -------->  |  v  |
60                                             [ `-' ]
70                                              `###'
80 print "how are you today";
90 input answer$
100 print "oh, that's too bad."
```

ADDITION A
```
110 print "why do you think you feel ";answer$;
120 input answer$
```

ADDITION B
```
Have fun adding more lines such as ...
   "did you ever have a cat"
   "were you ever dropped on your head"
   "now tell me about the pink bunnies"
   "and why do you think spiderman is after you"
```

Post-Program Questions

1. What symbol tells BASIC that your variable is going to be a word, not a number?

2. What does the command in line 20 do?

3. Did you have any problems inserting the ASCII art in your program?

4. Which key on the keyboard is right below the | (vertical line) character?

5. Did your program work correctly the first time? If not, what did you have to fix?

© Craig Whitmore, 2011

Worksheet 3 - Printing Variables

1. Fix (debug) the two errors in the program below:

```
10 primt "Happy Birthday!";
20 go to 10
```

2. What is the purpse of the semicolon ; in line 10 above?

3. What does this **next** program do in your own words?

```
10 input "how old are you";old
20 print "Wow!  You are ";old*12;" months old!"
```

4. If you ran the program and typed in "2", what would it print out? _____

5. What would adding line 30 do?
```
30 print "You are about ";old*12*365" days old"
```

6. What is the error in line 30 above? (You can circle it)

Notice in lines 20 and 30 above how the semicolons are used to place a variable (which can change each time) in a print line with text that doesn't change. The semicolon / quotation mark " ; or ; " tells BASIC that something is in that line that is not to be printed exactly as it's shown. The semicolon serves as a transition mark to help BASIC understand what we want it to do.

7. Consider line 40 below. What would it's output be on the screen?

```
40 print "You are old/10 decades old"
```

8. Rewrite line 40 in the space below so it's output is correct: _____

9. Looking at the program below, define what each of the four variables stands for:
    col$ =
    ani$ =
        =
        =

```
20 input "a color;col$
30 input  an animal";ani$
40 input "a movement"mov$
50 imput "a speed";spe$
```

10. Circle the 4 errors in the program above (one per line)

Program 3 - MadLibs

Madlibs are word games where a person is prompted for a list of words to substitute for blanks in a story. They were originally created in 1953 and often ask for literature terms such as nouns, verbs, adjectives (words describing a noun), and adverbs (words modifying verbs).

The program below asks for four separate variables: a color (adjective), an animal (noun), a movement (verb), and a speed (adverb).

```
10 rem Madlibs!!
20 input "a color";col$
30 input "an animal";ani$
40 input "a movement";mov$
50 input "a speed";spe$
60 print
70 print "The ";col$;" ";ani$;" was ";mov$;"ing ";spe$;"ly."
```

Type in and run the program. <u>Make at least two changes</u>, then save it as "madlibs.bas".

Post-Program Questions

1. How many variables are in this program?

2. What was the most difficult part of this program?

3. Why are the variables named the way they are?

4. Which character allows you to "glue" together all the variables in line 70?

5. Did your program work correctly the first time? If not, what did you have to fix?

ASCII ART ONLINE

Set-Up

1. Open Microsoft Word (or another wordprocessing program)
2. Set the font to "`Courier`" (any courier font is okay) This is a common mono-spaced font, which means that each character (. or O or M or |) takes up the same room on a line.
3. Type your name(s) at the top of the page.
4. Type **Step A, Step B, Step C** down the page
5. Ask your teacher if you are Saving or printing your document (if saving, save as "[your name] ASCII online")
6. Open Firefox (or another Web Browser)

Step A : Everyday Pictures (Simple ASCII Art)

1. Click on the address below or type it into the address bar.

    `http://llizard.cwahi.net/various other things.html`

2. Copy an ASCII art picture of each of the following onto your page. Use Edit-Copy, ⌘-C, or right click-copy to copy and Edit-Paste, ⌘-V, or right click-paste to paste. It is sometimes easier to copy online text if you click at the bottom of the ASCII picture and drag to highlight going up.

    a) door   b) angel   c) tree   d) chair

Step B : Words (Figlets)

1. Click on the address below or type it into the address bar.

    `http://www.network-science.de/ascii/`

2. In the "text" space type your first name.
3. Select "isometric" from the font list.
4. Click on "Do it!"
5. Scroll down the bottom window to see your name in ASCII art.
6. Copy your name to your document.

Step C : Animations

1. Click on the address below or type it into the address bar (it may take a few minutes to load).

    `http://www.asciimation.co.nz/`

2. In your document, type in 3 words that come to your mind when viewing this "asciimation".

Worksheet 4 - Creating ASCII Art

It is always best to create your ASCII art in a wordprocessing program first, then copy it to BASIC.

1. Open Word (or another wordprocessing program).
2. Make sure your font is changed to "Courier" or another mono-spaced font.
3. Create each of the following ASCII art pictures. (As you go along, periodically save your document as "ASCII art 1.doc")

    A) a stick figure.

    B) two advanced stick figures (feel free to use colored text)

    C) two common objects (house, car, heart, boat, rainbow)

    D) your first name, with the letters making the shapes

    * It sometimes helps to sketch out what you plan to create first, before you start typing.
    * Remember that ASCII art is really text, not a picture.

4. If you are printing out and turning in your work, put your name at the top of the page and the title "Worksheet 3 – ASCII Art".

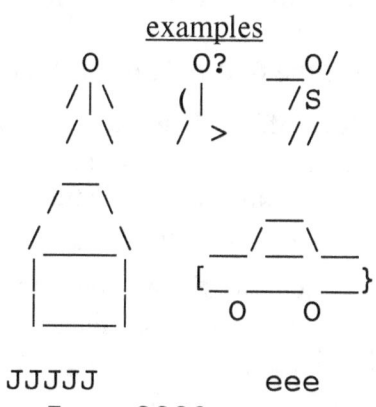

examples

```
    o        O?       _o/
   /|\      (|        /s
   / \      / >       //
```

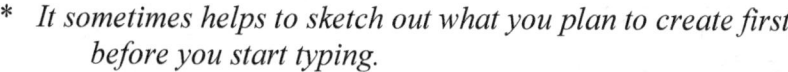

```
JJJJJ              eee
  J        0000   e   e
 J J       0  0   eeee
JJ         0000   eeee
```

Program 4 - ASCII Art in BASIC

The easiest way to use ASCII art in a basic program is to write your code in a **wordprocessor**, then copy and paste it into BASIC. This allows you to make changes quickly without having to worry about syntax errors as you work.

1. You need to **set the font to 'Courier'** (any type of 'courier' will do).
2. You need to **turn off the 'smart quotes'** that are enabled on most wordprocessors. (You can alternatively 'undo' the autoformatting every time you type a quote, but it's really easier to disable it all together.) The easiest way to turn off this autoformatting feature is to check the 'Help' function of your wordprocessor – just search for 'smartquotes' and it should tell you how to turn them on or off.
3. Start with the ASCII art picture you want to use. Remember, you can't use double quotes in your pictures (change them out for apostrophes). Also, every line in the ASCII art picture means one line of code in BASIC, so the larger the picture, the more programming you have to do.
4. At the start of the line, **type the line number, 'print' and a double quote**:

   ```
   20 print "  O
   ```

5. **Repeat this for each line** of your ASCII art:

   ```
   20 print "  O
   30 print "/|\
   40 print "/ \
   ```

6. Now **highlight the lines of code, copy them, and paste them into BASIC**. You may need to press the Return key (enter) two times to get to a clear command prompt.
7. Type **list** to check your program, then **run** it.
8. If everything works the way you want, **save** it to your Documents folder:

   ```
   >save "Documents/ascii art.bas"
   ```

Post-Program Questions

1. Why did we have you start working in a wordprocessing program first?

2. Do the error messages matter when you paste the ASCII art into BASIC?

3. What is the shortcut command for "print"?

4. Why is it a good idea to use small ASCII art pictures in BASIC programs?

5. Did your program work correctly the first time? If not, what did you have to fix?

Worksheet 5 - Basic Math

NAME_____

Remember, in BASIC we use the following symbols for math functions:

+ = add   − = subtract   ____ = multiply   ____ = divide

1. Type in the following commands and write out the answers on the lines:

    > print 121 + 296   _____

    > print 34 − 13   _____

    > print 54 * 73   _____

    > print 22 / 7   _____

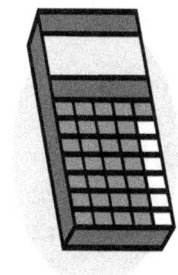

2. Now use Chipmunk Basic to find the answers to the following math problems:

    45*76 _____   54−23+8−74 _____   38+5−9*6 _____

    1093746−8374 _____   23.5/2+107 _____   8.5*3.2/7.1+4.9 _____

7. Create your own math problem for Chipmunk Basic to answer. Write it out in the space below (at least 10 numbers and use all four math symbols) and the answer that you get:

4. Five of the following are not formatted correctly. Cross out the mistakes and circle the correct one.

    (a) print 4,750,163   (d) print 612,5

    (b) print +−7567   (e) print 5,000

    (c) print 3.64.78   (f) print 2.3E10

Consider the following short program. (you may type it in if you wish, make sure you type "new" first)

```
10  x = 5
20  y = 8
30  z = x * y + x - y
```

5. What is the value for the variable 'z'? _____

6. Rewrite line 30 in the space below so that 'z' only equals the **sum** of 'x' and 'y'. _____

PROGRAM 5 • CALCULATOR

```
10 rem calculator program
20 a = 1
30 b = 3
40 print a+b
```

Addition A
```
40 print "a+b=";a+b
```

Addition B
```
20 input "a=";a
30 input "b=";b
```

Addition C
```
50 print "a-b=";a-b
60 print "axb=";a*b
70 print "a/b=";a/b
```

Challenge Addition
```
40 print a;"+ ";b;"= ";a+b
50 print a;"- ";b;"= ";a-b
60 print a;"x ";b;"= ";a*b
70 print a;"/ ";b;"= ";a/b
```

Post-Program Questions

1. Why can't we use a "x" for multiplication in BASIC?

2. What happens at line 70 if you put in '0' for variable 'b'?

3. What symboil do we usually use for dividing?   Why don't we use it in our program?

4. Are there any other math functions you can think of to use in BASIC?

5. Did your program work correctly the first time? If not, what did you have to fix?

Worksheet 6 - Looping

NAME _____

Looping is creating a recurring sequence of commands. The easiest one is the "for ... next" loop. Type in this short program.

```
10 for x = 1 to 10
20      print x
30 next x
40 print "done"
```

1. Explain what happens:

"For...next" loops can also be used to _____ down the computer.

2. Why would anyone want to slow their computer down?

Add in line 25 below then re-run your program.

```
25 for wait = 1 to 100000 : next wait
```

3. How did the program change this time? *(you may need to make the number 100000 smaller or larger depending on the processing speed of your computer)*

You can use this process to add numbers. Consider these modifications to the program:

```
20      y = y+x
...
40 print y
```

4. Now what happened?

5. What change would you make to add the numbers from 1 to 1000?

6. What is the sum of the numbers from 1 to 1000?

Finally, you don't have to just count up! Using the "step" command you can tell the computer to count by 2 or 5 or even count down by making the step a _____ number.

Modify line 10 in your current program to this:

```
10 for x = 1 to 100 step 5
```

7. How does it run differently?

8. How would you change line 10 to make the program count down by 10's from 1000 to 1?

© Craig Whitmore, 2011

Program 6 – Liftoff

```
10 rem rocket launch program
20 cls
30 print "Press RETURN to begin the countdown!"
40 input a$
50 for x = 10 to 1 step -1
60    print x
70    for wait = 1 to 100000 : next wait
80 next x
90 print "LIFTOFF"
```

You can also add an ASCII art rocket to the end of this program for more fun!
(The ... parts mean to add more lines!)

```
100 print "  A"
110 print " | |"
120 print " | |"
...
190 print "/|\"
200 print "@@@"
210 print "@@@"
...
```

Post-Program Questions

1. Which line number really makes this program work? Write it out below:

2. How many "for...next" loops are in this program?

3. Did you have to change your 'wait' time?   If so, which number worked best for you?

4. What purpose do you think the extra spaces in lines 60 and 70 serve?

5. Did your program work correctly the first time? If not, what did you have to fix?

Worksheet 7 - Conditional Statements

NAME _____

Fill in the BASIC math functions:
___ = add   ___ = subtract   ___ = multiply   ___ = divide

There are also symbols and terms in BASIC which are used to evaluate conditional statements:
> "greater than"   < "less than"   <> "does not equal"   and   or

A condition is a value that must be met for the program to proceed with the next command.
   Similar terms : provision, stipulation, prerequisite, limitation, qualification

---

Type in the following commands and the result that is displayed:
```
> print 5 = 8           _____
> print 6 = 2 * 3       _____
> print 2 * 4 = 10 - 2  _____
> print 100 * 100 > 999 + 999  _____
```

If the condition is true, BASIC returns a value of ____. If the condition is false, it returns ____.

In BASIC, we can also use the "if ... then ..." statement to check a condition.
Type in the following commands and record what is displayed (use "---" for nothing).

```
> if 20 > 10 then print "yes"       _____
> if 5 = 8 then print "yes"         _____
> if 2*9 > 5+10 then print "yes"    _____
```

Type in the following (it is NOT a program, simply a list of commands that BASIC does at once)
```
> a = 10
> b = 20
> c = 25
> if a + b = b - c then print "yes"   _____
> if c - b = a / 2 then print "yes"   _____
```

Input the small program below, then run it.
```
10 cls
20 input "what is 5 x 10"; x
30 if x = 50 then print "right"
```

Describe what the program above does: _____

_____

Circle the word in your description above that indicates the program is evaluating the condition.

Add a line 40 that will print "wrong" if x "does not equal" 50.

TEACHER'S INITIALS

Program 7 – Riddle Game

NAME _____

A **riddle** is a statement or question having a double or veiled meaning, put forth as a puzzle to be solved. A riddle can also be called an enigma, a paradox or a conundrum.

1. What kind of stones are never found in the ocean? _____
2. What building has the most stories? _____
3. If a fire hydrant has H2O inside, what does it have on the outside? _____
4. What is so fragile even saying its name can break it? _____
5. What 11-letter English word does everyone pronounce incorrectly? _____
6. What animal always knows the time? _____
7. I travel all over the world, but always stay in the corner. _____
8. What has 7 letters, it is greater than god, worse than the devil, poor people have it, rich people don't want it, and if you eat or drink it, you will die. _____
9. You can see me, and the more you take away the bigger I get. _____
10. What's always running but never moves? _____
11. If you turn me sideways, I am everything. If you cut my head off, I am nothing. _____
12. What is tall as a house, round as a cup, and all the kings horses can't draw it up? _____
13. What walks on four legs in the morning, two in the afternoon, and three at night? _____
14. What builds up castles and tears down mountains, makes some blind, but helps others see? _____
15. A box without hinge or lid, but golden treasure inside is hid. _____

Circle your favorite riddle from those above.

Create a Riddle Game Program <u>using at least 2 riddles</u>. A suggested code is shown below:

```
10 rem Riddle Game
20 input "why did the chicken cross the road:";answer$
30 if answer$= "to get to the other side" then goto 50
40 print "Nope!  Try again!" : goto 20
50 print "Great!  Here's the next riddle"
60 ...
```

Notice you could cut out a line by using:
```
30 if answer$<>"to get to the other side" then print "Nope!  Try again!" : goto 20
```

8, Dry, Egg, Hole, Human, Incorrectly, K9P, Library, Nothing, River, Sand, Silence, Stamp, Watchdog, Well

NAME_____

Worksheet 8 - RND (random) Numbers

1. What does "random" mean?

2. Type in "`print rnd(10)`" and press return. What number did you get? _____
   Now type the same command in again. What number did you get? _____

   Quit out of Chipmunk and then open it back up.
   Type in the same command twice more and record the numbers: _____ _____

3. Can a computer ever be truly "random"? Why or why not?

Using Chipmunk Basic, type in the following program.

```
10 x = rnd(10)
20 print x
30 goto 10
```

3. What happens when you **run** the program?

Code	Lowest #	Highest #
print rnd(10)		
print rnd(10)+1		
print rnd(10)+2		
print rnd(10)+11		

4. What is the purpose of adding "+1" to the code?

5. How would you change line 10 so that the program picks a number between 1 and 100?

6. If you wanted a number from 50 to 100, how should line 10 be written?

7. What if you wanted a number from 3 to 27?

8. In the space below, write a program to print out 5 randomly generated numbers.

© Craig Whitmore, 2011

PROGRAM 8 – NUMBER GUESSING GAME

```
10 rem number guessing
30 cls
40 print
50 number = 53
60 input "your guess – ";guess
100 print
110 if guess = number then goto 130
120 goto 60
130 print "you did it!"
```

ADDITION A
```
80 if guess < number then print "too low!"
90 if guess > number then print "too high!"
```

ADDITION B
```
50 number = rnd (100)+1
```

ADDITION C
```
20 tries = 0
70 tries = tries + 1
140 print "it took you ";tries;" guesses!"
```

Post-Program Questions

1. Why are there numbers missing from the first part of this program?

2. Without adding a random number, what would the answer always be?

3. Why do we add +1 in Addition B of line 50?

4. If you ran this program as shown above, what <u>one word</u> could you type in to always guess the correct number the first time?

5. Did your program work correctly the first time? If not, what did you have to fix?

Zork Introduction

Basic Idea of Game

Zork is one of the very first text adventure games. It was written between 1977-1979 by four MIT programmers. The name "Zork" is MIT hacker slang for an unfinished program. The game has no pictures, just words. There are three main levels: above ground, below ground, and the infamous maze.

The basic idea is to explore, find treasures, solve puzzles and defeat certain characters (the troll, cyclops, and thief). To save your progress type "save" and a dialogue box will appear. To load a saved game type "restore" and find your game. To restart from the beginning, type "restart". To have the game always tell you the description of each room (even when you've already been there) type "verbose". A score over 50 is good; over 90 is great; over 110 is difficult (unless you cheat and use the "how to win at Zork" instructions!). Have fun!

Common Commands to Use in Zork

- up (u)
- down (d)
- open
- get (all)
- light
- move

- enter
- inventory (i)
- eat
- drop
- kill

- give
- examine
- say
- wait
- again (to repeat last)

- north (n)
- south (s)
- east (e)
- west (w)
- also ne, nw, se, sw

First 16 Commands to Start the Game Off Right

1. N
2. E
3. Open
4. Enter
5. Get all
6. W
7. Get all
8. Light
9. E
10. U
11. Get all
12. D
13. W
14. Move rug
15. Open trap door
16. D

You can download Zork from www.infocom-if.org/downloads/downloads.html (interpreters available at www.csd.uwo.ca/Infocom/interp.html) or play online at pot.home.xs4all.nl/infocom/zork1.html
Maps can be found at www.lafn.org/webconnect/mentor/zork/zorkText.htm
A hintbook can be found at www.csd.uwo.ca/Infocom/Invisiclues/zork1/
A walkthrough of the game can be found at www.eristic.net/games/infocom/zork1.html

Some fun commands you might want to try are:
hello, zork, oil, xyzzy, plugh, chomp, count, win, listen, repent, what is …, smell, walk around, jump (try it several times just not in the kitchen or at the chasm!), kiss ground, talk to self

NAME _____

Zork Adventure Worksheet

(play online at pot.home.xs4all.nl/infocom/zork1.html)

goal of adventure (brief description – 2 to 5 lines):

6 things you might have <u>to do</u> in the story:

    1.

    2.

    3.

    4.

    5.

    6.

5 things you might have to pick up in the story:

    1.

    2.

    3.

    4.

    5.

2 ways the story could end:

    1.

    2.

In the space below, write out **2-5 sentences** telling what you think of this adventure game.

© Craig Whitmore, 2011

Choose-Your-Own-Adventure Rules

- You must have your adventure idea okay'ed by the teacher before you start programming it.
- You may not use real people in your game unless you get their approval first.
- The goal of your game may not be to shoot or kill people. So while you can make an army adventure, it needs to be one your 5-year-old brother could play. Or your principal. No assassinations.
- You may not make bloody, gory, killer zombie / vampire games. Sorry.
- You need to have 8 "rooms" and at least two ASCII art images.
- Each "room" should have at least two choices that go out from it.

Conventions

1) Use the variable "`choice$`" for basic inputs
2) Choices should be displayed in ALL CAPS **or** all lowercase
3) Include a "`rem`" or a "`print`" statement identifying each new "page" or "room"

Points Breakdown

500 points possible (450-A, 400-B, 350-C, 300-D)
    50 points per "page" or "room" (up to 8 "rooms")
    20 points each for two ASCII art pictures
    10 points for each extra ASCII art picture
    20 points for each extra variable used (other than choice$)
    20 points for each extra room

Adventure Ideas

Solve the robbery	Visit the future or past	Turn into an animal
Save the western town	Become part of a movie	Become a billionaire
Journey to another planet	Escape the castle	Become a superhero
Find the treasure	Discover a land of dinosaurs	Go to the school prom

And here are the titles of the first 20 original Choose-Your-Own-Adventure books:

1. The Cave of Time
2. Journey Under the Sea
3. By Balloon to the Sahara
4. Space and Beyond
5. The Mystery of Chimney Rock
6. Your Code Name is Jonah
7. The Third Planet from Altair
8. Deadwood City
9. Who Killed Harlowe Thrombey?
10. The Lost Jewels of Nabooti
11. Mystery of the Maya
12. Inside UFO 54-40
13. The Abominable Snowman
14. The Forbidden Castle
15. House of Danger
16. Survival at Sea
17. The Race Forever
18. Underground Kingdom
19. Secret of the Pyramids
20. Escape

© Craig Whitmore, 2011

#1
Choose Your Own Adventure Introduction

NAME _____

"Choose Your Own Adventure is a series of children's gamebooks ... Each story is written from a second-person point of view, with the reader ... making choices that determine the main character's actions in response to the plot and its outcome. ... For instance, the first decision offered in The Cave of Time is:

If you decide to start back home, turn to page 4.
If you decide to wait, turn to page 5.

After the reader makes a choice, the plot branches out ... leading to more decisions and eventually multiple possible endings." --- Wikipedia, 2008

In your own words, what is a Choose-Your-Own-Adventure?

What important BASIC commands will we use to program this kind of game?

In the spaces below, choose 2 adventure ideas that sound interesting to you, give them a title and describe them. Write out who the main character will be in 2-3 words. Describe the main goal or purpose of this adventure. List 6 things that might happen to the character as they go through this adventure. Write out 3 alternate endings to this story. (good, bad, ???)

---

1) _____

main character:

main goal:

6 things that might happen:

3 alternate endings:

---

2) _____

main character:

main goal:

6 things that might happen:

3 alternate endings:

© Craig Whitmore, 2011

#2

NAME _____

CHOOSE YOUR OWN ADVENTURE PROGRAM
FLOWCHART WORKSHEET

Flowchart Basics
- A flowchart can be thought of as a map of choices.
- Squares (or circles) show locations (either rooms or areas in a game).
- Choices are shown by arrows with words.

Consider the following simple flowchart:
    Fill in two choices along the arrows that lead to two possible endings.

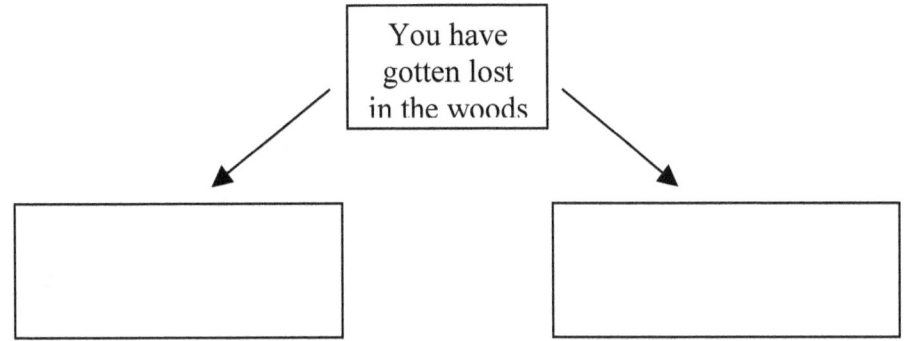

Pirate Treasure Flowchart
Play the game "Pirate Treasure" and fill out on your own. The first one is done for you.

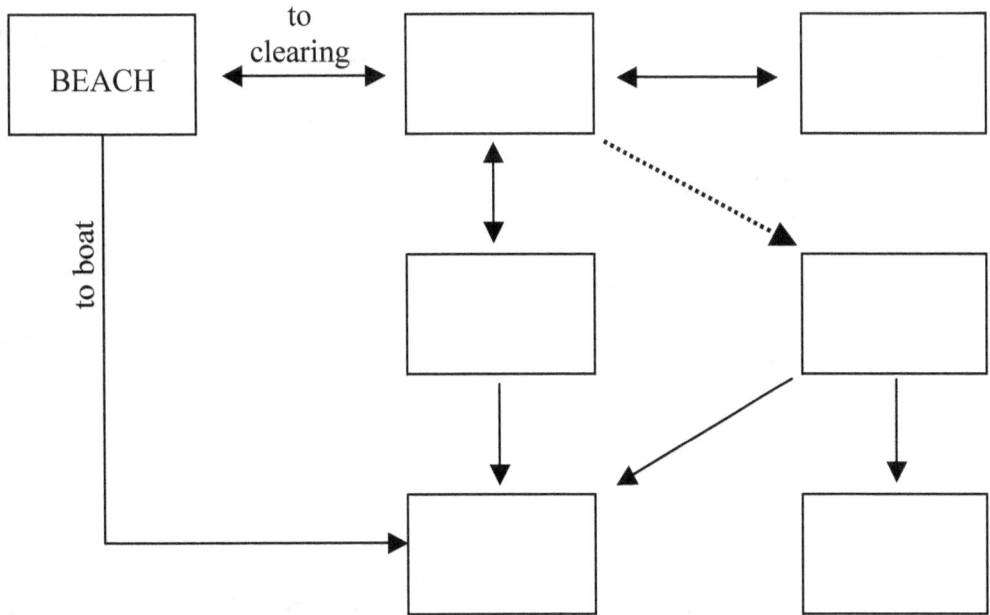

© Craig Whitmore, 2011

27

#3

NAME _____

Choose Your Own Adventure Program
Flowchart Planning

Possible Title _____

Adventure Description

    main character:

    main goal:

    6 things that happen:

    3 alternate endings:

Flowchart:

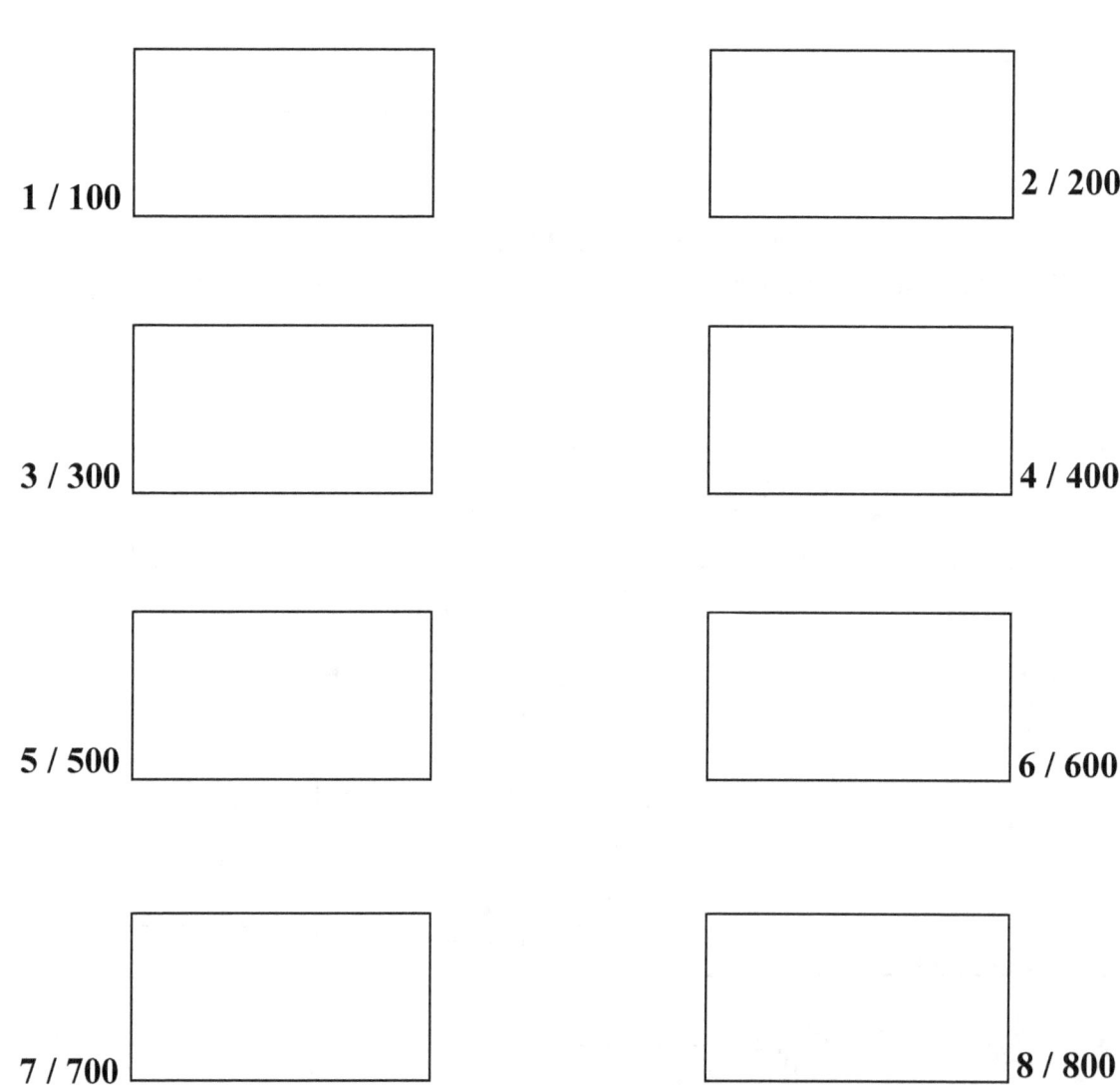

1 / 100   2 / 200

3 / 300   4 / 400

5 / 500   6 / 600

7 / 700   8 / 800

© Craig Whitmore, 2011

#4

100 rem _____
110 print
120 print " _____
130 print " _____
140 print "(_____) ";
150 input choice$
160 if choice$ = " _____ " then goto _____
170 if choice$ = " _____ " then goto _____
180 goto _____

200 rem _____
210 print
220 print " _____
230 print " _____
240 print "(_____) ";
250 input choice$
260 if choice$ = " _____ " then goto _____
270 if choice$ = " _____ " then goto _____
280 goto _____

300 rem _____
310 print
320 print " _____
330 print " _____
340 print "(_____) ";
350 input choice$
360 if choice$ = " _____ " then goto _____
370 if choice$ = " _____ " then goto _____
380 goto _____

© Craig Whitmore, 2011

400 rem _____

410 print

420 print " _____

430 print " _____

440 print "(_____) ";

450 input choice$

460 if choice$ = " _____ " then goto _____

470 if choice$ = " _____ " then goto _____

480 goto _____

500 rem _____

510 print

520 print " _____

530 print " _____

540 print "(_____) ";

550 input choice$

560 if choice$ = " _____ " then goto _____

570 if choice$ = " _____ " then goto _____

580 goto _____

600 rem _____

610 print

620 print " _____

630 print " _____

640 print "(_____) ";

650 input choice$

660 if choice$ = " _____ " then goto _____

670 if choice$ = " _____ " then goto _____

680 goto _____

NAME _____
PER ____ DATE _____

CYOA Mini-Quiz

/ 16

1. What was the name of the variable we all used?
   (a) time$, (b) x, (c) option$, (d) choice$, (e) choice

2. Which command checked to see which option the user picked?
   (a) rem, (b) if ... then, (c) goto, (d) chance, (e) random

3. Which command sent the program back if the user did not enter a correct option?
   (a) rem, (b) if ... then, (c) goto, (d) chance, (e) random

4. What was the name for the type of pictures we used?
   (a) jpegs, (b) UHU, (c) pngs, (d) gifs, (e) ASCII

5. Which command let you put comments in your program?
   (a) rem, (b) if ... then, (c) goto, (d) chance, (e) random

6. What did we use the semicolon - ; - for?
   (a) to leave a comment, (b) to keep things on the same line, (c) to clear the screen, (d) to put in art

7. Which command let the user enter a choice?
   (a) enter, (b) put, (c) input, (d) choice, (e) option

8. What is the name of the program we are using?
   (a) QBasic, (b) Pascal, (c) C++, (d) ChipmunkBasic, (e) Fortran

NAME _____
PER ____ DATE _____

CYOA Mini-Quiz

/ 16

1. What was the name of the variable we all used?
   (a) time$, (b) x, (c) option$, (d) choice$, (e) choice

2. Which command checked to see which option the user picked?
   (a) rem, (b) if ... then, (c) goto, (d) chance, (e) random

3. Which command sent the program back if the user did not enter a correct option?
   (a) rem, (b) if ... then, (c) goto, (d) chance, (e) random

4. What was the name for the type of pictures we used?
   (a) jpegs, (b) UHU, (c) pngs, (d) gifs, (e) ASCII

5. Which command let you put comments in your program?
   (a) rem, (b) if ... then, (c) goto, (d) chance, (e) random

6. What did we use the semicolon - ; - for?
   (a) to leave a comment, (b) to keep things on the same line, (c) to clear the screen, (d) to put in art

7. Which command let the user enter a choice?
   (a) enter, (b) put, (c) input, (d) choice, (e) option

8. What is the name of the program we are using?
   (a) QBasic, (b) Pascal, (c) C++, (d) ChipmunkBasic, (e) Fortran

© Craig Whitmore, 2011

NAME _____

CYOA Game Review

Review two games by playing them and answering the questions below.

Name of Game:

Goal of Game:

ASCII art pictures: _____   _____
                          _____   _____

Is this game easy or difficult?

What's one thing you like about this game?

What's one thing you would change about this game?

Did you win or lose?

Name of Game:

Goal of Game:

ASCII art pictures: _____   _____
                          _____   _____

Is this game easy or difficult?

What's one thing you like about this game?

What's one thing you would change about this game?

Did you win or lose?

Appendices

Programming Tips and Tricks

The Eight Stages of Game Programming

Stage 1 Vision – get an idea in mind, don't start off too grand, keep it simple, don't get bogged down in details (yet)

Stage 2 Planning – make a list, web diagram, and/or drawing about your game vision, what variables will you need

Stage 3 Blocking – block out the large "areas" of your program, set up a section for player movement, variable input, checking input, end of game, etc.

Stage 4 Programming – start filling in each "block", save often, save as different versions (ie. game1, game2) in case you program yourself into a corner and want to go back, play and fix as you go, remember to keep variables informative so you can easily remember what they stand for

Stage 5 Evaluation – step back, play it, think about it again, do you need to make it easier or more mysterious, is there an easier way to code it, will it make sense to someone else

Stage 6 Outside Critique – have a friend play and get their opinion, listen to them, listen to them, listen to them, what makes sense to you may be confusing to them

Stage 7 Repeat Stages 4 through 6 until satisfied with your product

Stage 8 Clean Up – add credits to your game, a Splash Screen to the start or end, cleanup any cumbersome code, rename the file with an interesting Game Title

PPPPP

There is an old saying that really holds true in programming: Prior Planning Prevents Poor Performance. The more you plan out ahead of time, the less problems you will deal with during programming which means you will usually finish your game much more quickly and it will turn out more the way you want it. Since there are usually several ways to program the same thing, the structure or shape of your programming can set you up for an elegant game or a waste of code. I usually write out my ideas on paper first, then start coding on the computer after I have a broad picture. Whichever method you find works best for you remember, prior planning prevents poor performance. (It's even an example of alliteration, for your English language development!)

ADVANCED TEXT-ADVENTURE GAMES

This is a **much** more advanced way of programming. Over the years I have taught it to a few students who were ready for this, either because they had taken a programming class before or because they just seemed to "get" the basic programming concepts better than most. I suggest reading through this whole section before you start programming to make sure you understand the whole concept. New commands for this method include `mid$` and `dim`, and a new concept is the array (and/or matrix).

Section Contents
    Overview
    Step 1: Map Design
        Movement Option 1: Using an Intermediate Variable
        Movement Option 2: Using a Preset Variable
    Step 2: Preloading Information Variables
    Example Game Code (Options 1 and 2)

Overview

This method makes use of array (or matrix) programming. An array is an arrangement of information in rows and columns, basically a square (A matrix adds depth to it, so it's more like a cube or 3D). We use a numerical location variable ("lo") and preloaded room variables (a$, b$, c$, etc.). So the array can be visualized like this:

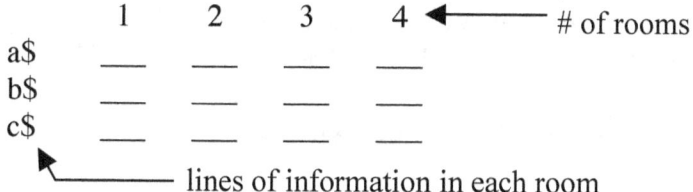

Each "room" will have lines of information that are the letter variables and the number shows how many rooms there are. So the above example would have four rooms and three lines of information for each room. As the player types in a direction to move, the game adds or subtracts from "lo" (the "room" number) and prints the new room information (the letter variables). The correct way to access the first room variable would be `a$(1)` and the lower right-hand one would be `c$(4)`. Notice that this is not a map of the game, but a "map" of the information that will be displayed in each "room".

Step 1 : Map Design

Plan out a numeric map: Let the variable **lo** be their current location.

                                                        (lo=lo-10)
    1 — 2 — 3   Up
    11 — 12 — 13 |
    21 — 22 — 23   (lo=lo-1) Left — lo — Right (lo=lo+1)
                                                            |
                                                          Down
                                                        (lo=lo+10)

It is important to note that the actual game-map doesn't have to be left/right or north/south even though the programming map uses those conventions. For example, you could have a space adventure where they land on different planets that are far apart. The map shows how the choices are connected within the game.

One drawback of this design is that you can't really have a map with more than 10 rooms across (left – right), since they would wrap to the next level down. (But if your adventure is that large, you probably need a higher level language to program in!)

You could even get really complex and have a three dimensional (3D) map setup like a cube:

```
    51— 52— 53
   / | / |  / |     where up/down is +/- 10, left/right is +/- 1
  1 — 2 — 3  |      and back/forward is +/- 50.
  | 61— 62— 63      (This is picture of what a matrix (3 dimensional)
  | / | / | /       would look like as opposed to an array (2 dimensional).)
  11— 12— 13
```

Another issue with either a 2D or 3D map like this is that you have to check to make sure the player doesn't "walk off" the map into nothingness. There are two methods that work well: using an intermediate variable or using a preset variable.

Movement Option 1 – using an intermediate variable

With this option, you use a variable other than "`lo`" and a series of if...then... statements to check if the planned move is out of bounds. If it is an okay move, you assign the planned location ("`lonext`") to "`lo`". The code below is for a map with six rooms, 1-3 and 11-13.

```
100 input choice$
110 if choice$="right" then lonext = lo + 1          ← assigns intermediate variable (lonext)
...
150 if lonext < 1 then print "you can't go that way" : goto 100
160 if lonext > 3 and lonext < 11 then print "you can't go that way" : goto 100    ← checks for out-of-bounds
170 if lonext > 13 then print "you can't go that way" : goto 100
180 lo = lonext          ← if move is allowable, assigns lonext to lo
```

This can get cumbersome when checking for out-of-bounds and it is easy to get confused with the greater-than / less-than signs.

Movement Option 2 – using a preset variable

This option is more elegant but also more complex. It involves the use of a string command, `mid$`. Here is the diagram of the command:

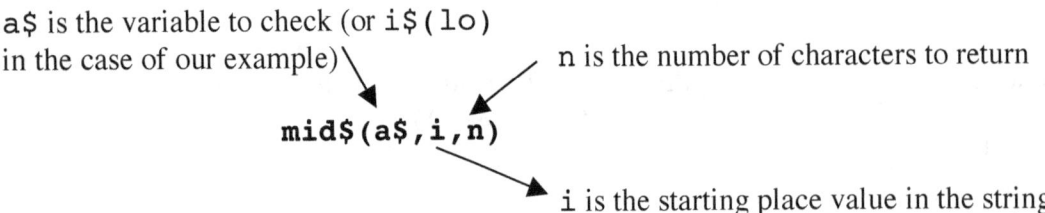

a$ is the variable to check (or i$(lo) in the case of our example)

n is the number of characters to return

mid$(a$,i,n)

i is the starting place value in the string

With this option, you preset a variable for each room showing in which directions movement is allowed. A '+' shows allowed movement, a '-' shows unallowed movement. A general direction convention to use is

```
       left, right, up, down
       
    30 i$(1) = "-+-+"
```

In our example, each movement variable will have four characters. If `mid$(i$(lo),1,1)="+"` then the player can move to the left. Again, while is more complex, but it makes the creation of large maps much easier.

An additional benefit is that it also allows for the modification of the map during gameplay by simply changing the data in `i$(lo)`. For instance, if pulling a lever opens a hidden door to the left, you can change i$ from "`----`" to "`+---`" to allow them to move through the newly opened door.

An example code is shown below:

```
30  i$(1) = "-+-+"
40  i$(2) = "++-+"
50  i$(3) = "+--+"
60  i$(11) = "-++-"
70  i$(12) = "+++-"
80  i$(13) = "+-+-"
...
100 input choice$
110 if choice$ = "left" and mid$(i$(lo),1,1) = "+" then lo = lo-1
120 if choice$ = "right" and mid$(i$(lo),2,1) = "+" then lo = lo+1
130 if choice$ = "up" and mid$(i$(lo),3,1) = "+" then lo = lo-10
140 if choice$ = "down" and mid$(i$(lo),4,1) = "+" then lo = lo+10
```

Lines 30-80: preload movement variable i$ for rooms 1-3 and 10-13 using the left, right, up, down convention

Lines 110-140: checking allowable movement using mid$ and assigning new location if ok

Step 2: Preloading Information Variables

To make a truly playable game, you'll need information to display for each room. By preloading the information about each room into a variable, you can automatically display the correct information when they move from room to room. You can also modify the information as the gameplay progresses.

First, you need to decide how many lines of information you want to display for each room. This should be the same number for each room. It's nice to have a room title (LIBRARY or SATURN) and at least 2-3 lines of information about each room. You may also want to include ASCII art (which can get more complicated, but really adds to the gameplay).

For example, if you have five lines of information, designate the variables a – e to hold that information. You will dimension (the command is **dim**) each variable (a$, b$, c$, d$, e$) to have as many subsets as you have room numbers (such as (a$(1), a$(2), a$(3), and so on). Some of the dimensioned subsets may remain unused.
Here is an example of a 24-room map with only 2 lines of informatino for each room:

```
10 rem setup each room's info
20 dim a$(24), b$(24)
```

Next, you load the desired information into each variable.

```
1000 rem room info
1010 a$(1)="You are in the upper left room"
1020 b$(1)="This room is #1"
1030 a$(2)="You are in the upper middle room"
1040 b$(2)="This room is #2"
1050 a$(3)="You are in the upper right room"
1060 b$(3)="This room is #3"
...
1130 goto 70
```

Example Game Code 1 (with an Intermediate Variable for Movement)

```
10 rem setup each room's info
20 dim a$(13), b$(13) : lo=1              ← Dim(ension) each variable
30 goto 1000                              ← It's customary to read in or set the room
70 rem print new room info                  data at the end of your program
80 cls
90 print a$(lo) : print b$(lo)            ← Print current room info
100 rem input their move
110 input choice$                         ← Input desired move
120 rem set their move
130 if choice$ = "left" then lonext = lo - 1    ⎫
140 if choice$ = "right" then lonext = lo + 1   ⎬ Set intermediate location
150 if choice$ = "up" then lonext = lo - 10     ⎪
160 if choice$ = "down" then lonext = lo + 10   ⎭
170 rem check their move
180 if lonext < 1 then goto 70                  ⎫
190 if lonext > 3 and lonext <11 then goto 70   ⎬ Check desired move
200 if lonext > 13 then goto 70                 ⎭
210 rem make their move
220 lo=lonext                             ← Set new location
230 goto 70
1000 rem room info
1010 a$(1)="You are in the upper left room"     ⎫
1020 b$(1)="This room is #1"
1030 a$(2)="You are in the upper middle room"
1040 b$(2)="This room is #2"
1050 a$(3)="You are in the upper right room"
1060 b$(3)="This room is #3"
1070 a$(11)="You are in the lower left room"    ⎬ Read in all data for each room
1080 b$(11)="This room is #11"
1090 a$(12)="You are in the lower middle room"
1100 b$(12)="This room is #12"
1110 a$(13)="You are in the lower right room"
1120 b$(13)="This room is #13"                  ⎭
1130 goto 70
```

An example of the gameplay is below:

```
You are in the upper left room
This room is #1
? right
You are in the upper middle room
This room is #2
? right
You are in the upper right room
This room is #3
? down
You are in the lower right room
This room is #13
? left
You are in the lower middle room
This room is #12
? left
You are in the lower left room
This room is #11
? down
You are in the lower left room
This room is #11
```

And here is a "map" of the game's rooms.

#1	#2	#3
#11	#12	#13

© Craig Whitmore, 2011

Example Game Code 2 (with a Preset Variable for Movement)

```
10 rem setup each room's info
20 dim a$(13), b$(13), i$(13) : lo=1        ←———— Dim(ension) each variable
30 goto 1000   ←———————————————————————————— It's customary to read in or set the
70 rem print new room info                         room data at the end of your program
80 cls
90 print a$(lo) : print b$(lo)   ←—————————— Print current room info
100 rem input their move
110 input choice$   ←——————————————————————— Input desired move
120 rem set their move
130 if choice$ = "left"  and mid$(i$(lo),1,1) = "+" then lo = lo - 1  ⎫
140 if choice$ = "right" and mid$(i$(lo),2,1) = "+" then lo = lo + 1  ⎬ Check and set
150 if choice$ = "up"    and mid$(i$(lo),3,1) = "+" then lo = lo - 10 ⎪    new location
160 if choice$ = "down"  and mid$(i$(lo),4,1) = "+" then lo = lo + 10 ⎭
170 goto 70
1000 rem room and movement info
1010 a$(1)="You are in the upper left room"
1020 b$(1)="This room is #1"
1030 a$(2)="You are in the upper middle room"
1040 b$(2)="This room is #2"
1050 a$(3)="You are in the upper right room"
1060 b$(3)="This room is #3"
1070 a$(11)="You are in the lower left room"
1080 b$(11)="This room is #11"
1090 a$(12)="You are in the lower middle room"   ⎫———— Read in all data for each room
1100 b$(12)="This room is #12"
1110 a$(13)="You are in the lower right room"
1120 b$(13)="This room is #13"
1130 i$(1)  = "-+-+"
1140 i$(2)  = "++-+"
1150 i$(3)  = "+--+"
1160 i$(11) = "-++-"
1170 i$(12) = "+++-"
1180 i$(13) = "+-+-"
1190 goto 70
```

© Craig Whitmore, 2011

Description of Mr. Whitmore's Games

All of Mr. Whitmore's Text-Adventure games (though copyrighted) are available to download free of charge at
http://norris.k12.ca.us/schools/nms/index.cfm?fuseaction=class&class_id=7

```
22 print "     __     ___   _      __     _ _  ___   ___   ___                    "
24 print "    /_\   (_ _)( )    /_\   ( \( )(_ _)(_ _)/ __)"
26 print "   /(_)\   )(  )(_   /(_)\   )  (   )(  _)(_ \__ \"
28 print "  (__)(__)(__) (____)(__)(__)(_)\_) (__) (____)(___/"
30 print "     __    ___    _    ___   _ _   ___    ___    ___   _   _    ___     "
32 print "    /_\  (  _ \( /) (  _)( \( )(  _ )(  )(  )(  _ \(  _)"
34 print "   /(_)\   )(_) )\ /   )_)  )  (   )(_) )(  )  /  )_)  "
36 print "  (__)(__)(____/  \/   (___)(_)\_)  (__) (_____)(_)\_)(___) "
```

Total lines:	606
Type of game:	linear
Goal of game:	discover the lost city of Atlantis
ASCII art:	every room
Difficulty:	medium

There is only one "good" ending and several "bad" endings to this adventure. It is a linear game, where the player moves in one direction only, so there is no need for a dimensioned array. Each "room" has associated ASCII art and several easter eggs (taking pictures, reading the book) are included. Line 352 shows an interesting BASIC conditional command: on x goto …. It's a quick way to check and send on when the input will be a sequential number (in this case, 1 to 7). The "if ext = 0" statements scattered through the program make sure that the program doesn't repeat itself when special commands (map, read book, take picture) are used. There are also clues hidden in some of the ASCII art, as shown in line 1420 of the code below (the arrow pointing left):

```
1400 map = 5 : cls : print "                        FORK IN THE TUNNEL"
1405 print ".`~-._---    -- _,~. Following the fish leads you"
1410 print "  .   \ -   -/  .   through a small tunnel deep"
1415 print "    (   )-     ;  . into the cave.  As the water"
1420 print "  ) )  ;<- - (    ( clears, you see two tunnels"
1425 print "( (   : -    \  ) ) branching off to the left"
1430 print "  ) ) /  -   / (  ( and the right.  The small"
1435 print "( _.' --     `~-. ) fish seems to have dis-"
1445 print ",~  .,, .,,. ,., \  appeared somewhere."
1450 print : print "A"; : input choice$
1452 gosub 3400
1455 if choice$ = "left" then goto 1500
1460 if choice$ = "right" then goto 2700
1465 if ext = 0 then print "I'm sorry I don't understand"
1467 if ext = 1 then ext = 0
1470 goto 1450
```

Some special choices that need to be available in each area are worth noting. The "gosub / return" commands (line 1452) allow easy checking of these special choices from any area. Typing "map" shows the parts of the game the player has gone to up to that point. "Reading the book" shows the commands to win in reverse. Typing "blub blub" (talking like a fish) allows the player to "teleport" to any of ten various areas of the game.

```
2860 print "WELCOME TO ADVENTURE CASTLE"
2870 print ""
2880 print "                      |~"
2890 print "                      |~"
2900 print "                     /_\"
2910 print "            |~|#|_|~"
2920 print "         |~/_\|  |#|__|~          |~"
2930 print "        /_\|#| |#|/__/_\._._._.|"
2940 print "        |#||_||_|___|#|...-...|"
2950 print "        |......-......|  |#|   |"
2960 print "        \|  [ ] |#|  [ ] | |__|#|__|~~~~~"
2970 print " ~~~~~~|____|#|____|/"
```

Total lines:	377
Type of game:	non-linear, dimensioned array, intermediate location variable
Goal of game:	become the new king
ASCII art:	every room
Difficulty:	easy

The goal of this game is to find the crown, put it on, release the dragon, and become the new king (or queen). The game uses a dimensioned array with eight variables for each room. "Walking off the map" is controlled by using an intermediate location variable (lon). Each room has associated ASCII art and several times clues are in the ASCII art to help in the game are hidden in the ASCII art (rooms 11 and 22). The first task (entering the castle) uses a riddle from Tolkien's "Lord of the Rings" trilogy.

Lines 70-630 setup the basic room information. Lines 640-990 input and check commands and movement. Typing my youngest son's name (jarren) allows teleporting around the castle. Typing "hint" will give you help with whichever room you are in while typing "help" will give you an overall idea of what you must do to win.

```
70   a$(11) = "     _ _ _         "    WEST TOWER"
80   b$(11) = "|‾|_|‾|_|‾|_|‾| |  "
90   c$(11) = "T     _  _  _     |"    You are in the tallest tower of the castle."
100  d$(11) = "E_        |  |  _/"     You can see the whole countryside stretching"
110  e$(11) = "   |_  _|_|    _|"      out below you from the tower window.  Rich"
120  f$(11) = "     N_    _   _/"      tapestries cover the walls, telling fanciful"
130  g$(11) = "      |_  _  _|"        tales of ancient times.  A spiral staircase"
140  h$(11) = "        |  _  |"        leads down."

310  a$(22) = "   ||    ||    ,-~~-.  "    THRONE ROOM"
320  b$(22) = "   ||  X|    / ,::. \  "
330  c$(22) = "   ||  I|   :  ,'_'. :"    You have found the throne of the king.  It"
340  d$(22) = "   ||  V|   |:::::::::|"    seems to glow with an inner light, inviting"
350  e$(22) = "   ||   ||  ||:::::::||"    you to sit on its luxurious seat.  You see"
360  f$(22) = "   ::  ;;  (_):::::::(_) exits to the left and the right."
370  g$(22) = "   \\//     ;_'----'_:  "
380  h$(22) = "   ___'____(__)____(_)_"

910 if mov$ = "down" then lon = lo+10
920 if mov$ = "up" then lon = lo-10
930 if mov$ = "right" then lon = lo+1
940 if mov$ = "left" then lon = lo-1
950 if lon < 11 or lon > 13 and lon < 21 or lon > 23 and lon < 31 or lon > 33
then goto 1000
960 lo = lon
```

```
2030 print "                _____              ___       _           "
2040 print "   _____    /  /  /___   _____ /  /___   (_)_____ "
2050 print "  /  _/ __/   /  /  //  _/ /  ____/  / ___/  / // __   __/"
2060 print " /  /__>  </  /  /  //  /  (  (___/  (__  ) / // _/ / /   "
2070 print "/_____/_/|_|\__/\__//__/_____/\__/___/\_/_//_/  /_/    "
```

Total lines:	333
Type of game:	non-linear, dimensioned array
Goal of game:	fix the starship and defeat the aliens
ASCII art:	almost none
Difficulty:	difficult

    This game is a Star Trek-style adventure. It is probably the most difficult of the text-games I have written. It starts as your captain explains the current problem. An alien ship has pulled you out of warp and damaged the Excelsior. You are given a phaser and sent to fix the ship and save everyone from the alien menace. The only ASCII art is the ship map shown by typing "map" or by examining certain walls for more detail (locations 14 and 22).

    Several tasks must be finished before you can transport over to the alien ship and win the game, including finding the doctor's tricorder, patching a cable, and turning on the transporter. It is possible (1740) to transport yourself into empty space. The score adds up as you complete various tasks. Typing "score" displays your current score and number of moves (*ala* "Zork"). You can win the game (in order of increasing score) by destroying the alien ship, shooting the alien captain, or demanding his surrender.

    The game uses a dimensioned array for tracking movement, though not a preset movement variable. Lines 810 – 970 check automatic responses depending on location and variable values. Lines 980 – 1240 allow and check player input. Lines 1560-1660 checks all of the multiple "push button" possibilities depending on your current location.

    Fun parts of the game: Secret messages (in backwards LEET) are on the walls of the alien ship. Line 610 says "I like Johnny Depp". Line 670 displays "Flood bad Halo bad". Line 760 shows "ZYXXY" in a nod to the first text-adventure game, "Colossal Cave Adventure". Once again, typing "becca" (my younges daughter's nickname) (990) fulfills all the requirements to win the game. Typing my other childrens' names (Kayleigh, Tyler, Zachary and/or Jarren) tells you something about them. Pressing "b" when the game ends allows you to keep on playing (this was actually a leftover diagnostic-style command that I forgot to take out when I was finished programming this game).

```
660 a$(17) = "--ALIEN MAIN PASSAGE MID--"
670 b$(17) = "You seem to be in the middle of the alien ship's main passage.  A
message is scrawled on the wall 'b4d ol4H b4d bool7'."
680 c$(17) = "You can probably move fore or aft along this main passage."

1420 rem map of ship
1430 print : print "               _____                   _-_"
1440 print "          \==___.___.___._/             __.---'---`---.___"
1450 print "                   \_\                 \___.___.___.____----/"
1460 print "                     \ \               /  /            `-_-'"
1470 print "                      \ `--_____~'     '."
1480 print "                      /___.___.___.___.___  ~||"
1490 print "                     `___.___.___.___.___,-'"
1500 print : goto 980
1510 print
1520 print "COMMANDS:"
1530 print "up, down, fore, aft, l(ook), i(nventory), get ---, push ---, map,
help, score"
1540 print : print "Type 'commands' to see these again."
1550 get y$
1560 return
```

```
2160 print "   ____     .  __           __       _____                                         "
2170 print "\  \   |  |/ /  _____   _/  |_  ____       _/  |_____    _____ _ _____   "
2180 print " _____  \ |   / \\   __\/ __ \     \   __\_  __ \ _____  \  /  ___// | \_  __ \  "
2190 print "    |    |   \|     <  |  |  \  ___/       |  |  |  | \/\  ___/ / __ \_\___ \\  |  /|  | \/ "
2200 print "    |____|___ /___|_ \ |__|   \___  >      |__|  |__|    \___  >____  /____  >__|    |__|   "
2210 print "             \/     \/            \/                         \/     \/     \/              "
```

Total lines:	233
Type of game:	non-linear, basic code example
Goal of game:	find the pirate treasure
ASCII art:	every room
Difficulty:	easy

This was actually the first text adventure game I wrote as an example for my first programming classes. This is the second version of it, with more ASCII art added. The goal of the game is to find the pirates' buried treasure before they find you. I think this is the simplest and cleanest of all the games described here.

It is a non-linear game, but it does not use a dimensioned array, just allows you to move back and forth from connected areas. The two jobs you must complete to win are picking up the shovel on the hill (and climbing the tree in the clearing to find your way to Skull Rock. A progressive map shows where you have bene on the island. There is a maze of vines (1700-1950) which is pretty easy, although the pirates can (randomly) catch you. There are two ways for the game to end: the pirates find you (Oh no!) or you get the buried treasure (Yeah!).

Typing "becca" (my youngest daughter's nickname) fulfills all the requirements and sends you to Skull Rock to win the game. The "say" commands are rem'ed out (1480 and 1610) – they only work on the Macintosh version.

```
 90 print "                   |"
100 print "                  \ _ /"
110 print "                -= (_) =-"
120 print "                 /   \           _\/_"
130 print "                   |           //o\  _\/_"
140 print "   _____ _ __ ___ _  |    _    _ |   _/o\\  _"
150 print " =-=-_-_-__=_-=_=_===_,-'|'  ' ""-|-,_ "'"
160 print "    =-  _===-_-===_,-'' |'''"
170 print "       =- == -=.--" ""
180 print "You are standing on the beach.  Sand and water stretch in all directions."
190 print "You see a boat farther along the shore and a clearing through the forest."
200 print "You have a parchment to draw a map on as you go (type 'map' to see it)."
210 print "(boat - clearing) ";
220 input choice$
230 if choice$ = "boat" then goto 1540
240 if choice$ = "clearing" then goto 280
250 if choice$ = "map" then gosub 1960
260 if choice$ = "becca" then tree$ = "yes" : shovel = 1 : clearing = 1 : hill = 1 : goto 1100
270 goto 210

1960 rem map
1970 map = map+1
1980 print
1990 print " ,~~~~~~~~~~~~~~~~~~~~,"
2000 print "(      Beach          ("
2010 if clearing = 1 then print " )         |           )"
2020 if clearing = 1 then print "(          |           ("
2030 if hill = 1 then print " ) Clearing----Hill    )"
2040 if hill = 0 and clearing = 1 then print " ) Clearing            )"
2050 if tree$ = "yes" then print "(         |   `-.       ("
2060 if tree$ = "yes" then print " \        |     `~~.     \"
2070 if tree$ = "yes" then print "  )    Tree      .~'     )"
2080 if tree$ = "no" and hill = 1 then print "(                      ("
2090 if tree$ = "no" and hill = 1 then print " \                      \"
2100 if tree$ = "no" and hill = 1 then print "  )                      )"
2110 if tree$ = "yes" or hill = 1 then print " (        Skull Rock("
2120 print " '~~~~~~~~~~~~~~~~~~~~'"
2130 print : return
```

the map changes based on where the player has been

© Craig Whitmore, 2011

```
 80 print "                    __                __              "
 90 print "      _____ ____   /_/ ____ _ ___  __/_/ __  __ _____ "
100 print "     ( _-</ __ \/ // / / __ `// _ \/ /\ // / / // ___/"
110 print "    /___/ .__/\_, /  \_,_/\_,_/|___/_//_/\_,_,_//_/    "
120 print "       /_/   /___/"
```

Total lines:	931
Type of game:	linear / non-linear, dimensioned matrix, preset movement variable
Goal of game:	stop Mr. X from carrying out his plans
ASCII art:	every room
Difficulty:	difficult

In this adventure the player is a secret agent. Your mission is to apprehend "Mr. X" and stop his terrorist plans. This game is a mix of linear and non-linear gameplay. The first 400 lines are fairly linear. Once the player gets underground into the base, the game uses a dimensioned matrix of variables to display the information for each room. Movement is controlled by a preset variable (i$) (5000-5140), which allows changes in allowed movement throughout the gameplay. This also allows the rooms themselves to change as the game is played. For example, in room 14, a message appears on the wall when the lightbulb is turned on.

Score is kept as you play. There are several additional things that must occur to receive the highest score. Lines 530-990 check the various possible input commands. "Look" (740) reprints the room description. Notice (6440) that the variable "keey" is used instead of "key" because the word "key" is a reserved word in BASIC and not allowed as a variable name. An alarm is also included, where various wrong choices can lead to its going off. Once in the underground base, a random code tells you to hide when you hear footsteps.

The game can end in one of two ways: you can fail your mission (but still survive) or succeed (but to various degrees). Lines 6340-6690 provide a summary of your gameplay as well as a "final spy rank" based on the numerical score. Of course, the highest rank possible is "James Bond, 007". The end of the game (though not the program) (8280-8380) is an attempt at scrolling credits.

There are several fun additions to this program. Each room's "carpet" is a different keyboard character, which is meant to help in navigating the underground base. Each carpet is also described in a different manner ("truly hideous", "revolting", "interesting") in an attempt at humor. The "read book" command (710) makes use of some interesting reading (Doctor Seuss, Charge of the Light Brigade, Sonnet 116). Reading the right page also provides the answer to the two mazes. The mazes themselves (5590-5820) are an interesting way to include a graphic element in a text-adventure game. Lines 8400-8970 provide one of three an animated shows when the player looks in the window of room 7. The code "taramarie" (720) (my wife's name) allows teleporting around the game. The code "rebekahanne" (730) (my youngest daughter's name) fulfills all of the mission parameters.

```
3580 a$(7) = " -|-|------------------"
3590 b$(7) = ",||-|   __    ----  -"
3600 c$(7) = ",||-|-[_~_]  |   |  |"
3610 d$(7) = ",||-|    __  /_/  |  |"
3620 e$(7) = ",||-|   |0.||_____|  |"
3630 f$(7) = ",||-|___|0.||_____|"
3640 g$(7) = ",|/,,,,.__|/,,,,:/"
3650 h$(7) = "---------------------"
3660 j$(7) = "right, up, open safe, read sign"
3670 k$(7) = "You've found the entrance to an underground complex!  There is a (locked) safe, "
3680 l$(7) = "a sign on the wall and a window.  The carpet is yellow.  Exits lead up and to the right."
```
} each room is shown in a semi-3D view which allows quite a bit of detail including exits and simple objects.

```
5590 rem maze1
5600 cls
5610 print " _____ "
     print ">___| a|  _|_ 4 |"  :
     print "|  | |__|b__ |  |"  :
5620 print "| _|1|__ c|_|_|  |"  :
     print "| |__|_|_|d|   |"  :
     print "|e    f  |g_   |"  :
5630 print "|__3|____h|2|_|i|"  :
     print "|_____|____>"
```
} these lines are shown here in an expanded form to show the shape of the maze – the correct way through it (from start (>) through 1-4 to the exit (>)) is **efba1abfh2hfe3efbcgd4di**

© Craig Whitmore, 2011

Answers for Teachers (Selected Worksheets)

Worksheet 1 - Basic Commands Practice

Part B – 1. Macintosh: apple - . (command - .)   Windows/Linux: ctrl – c or ctrl – z

Worksheet 2 - Inputting Variables

Inputting is allowing the user to enter __data__ that the program uses for calculations. It involves the use of __variables__. The variables can be one of two types:

Variable name	Data type	Sign or symbol	Examples
Numerical	Numbers	---	x, y, num, car, color, cat
String	Text (words)	$	x$, name$, car$, dog$

Worksheet 5 - Basic Math

+ = add   – = subtract   __*__ = multiply   __/__ = divide

Worksheet 6 - Looping

"For…next" loops can also be used to __slow__ down the computer.

2. Why would anyone want to slow their computer down?   Because they operate so quickly, we can't keep up.

5. What change would you make to add the numbers from 1 to 1000?   10 for x = 1 to 1000

6. What is the sum of the numbers from 1 to 1000?   500,500

Finally, you don't have to just count up! Using the "step" command you can tell the computer to count by 2 or 5 or even count down by making the step a __negative__ number.

Worksheet 7 - Conditional Statements

If the condition is true, BASIC returns a value of __1__. If the condition is false, it returns __0__.

Program 7 – Riddle Game

1. dry
2. library
3. K9P (canine pee)
4. silence
5. incorrectly
6. watch dog
7. stamp
8. nothing
9. hole
10. iver
11. 8
12. well (from *Zork II*)
13. human (Riddle of the Sphinx)
14. sand
15. egg (from *The Hobbit*)

Worksheet 8 - RND (random) Numbers

3. Can a computer ever be truly "random"? Why or why not?   No. It had to be programmed to pick a "random number" so it's not truly random. There is a pattern.

4. What is the purpose of adding "+1" to the code?   So the computer starts counting at 1 instead of 0.

5. How would you change line 10 so that the program picks a number between 1 and 100?   10 x = rnd(100)+1

6. If you wanted a number from 50 to 100, how should line 10 be written?   10 x = rnd (51)+50

7. What if you wanted a number from 3 to 27?   10 x = rnd(25)+3

© Craig Whitmore, 2011

Choose Your Own Adventure Program
Flowchart Worksheet

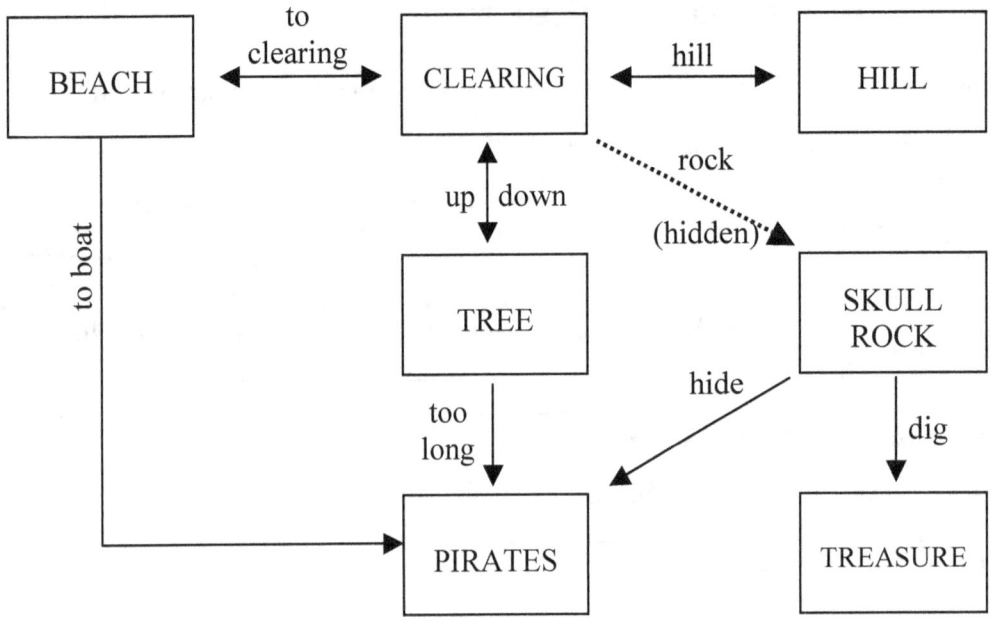

CYOA Mini-Quiz

1. What was the name of the variable we all used?
   (a) time$, (b) x, (c) option$, **(d) choice$,** (e) choice

2. Which command checked to see which option the user picked?
   (a) rem, **(b) if ... then,** (c) goto, (d) chance, (e) random

3. Which command sent the program back if the user did not enter a correct option?
   (a) rem, (b) if ... then, **(c) goto,** (d) chance, (e) random

4. What was the name for the type of pictures we used?
   (a) jpegs, (b) UHU, (c) pngs, (d) gifs, **(e) ASCII**

5. Which command let you put comments in your program?
   (a) rem, (b) if ... then, (c) goto, (d) chance, (e) random

6. What did we use the semicolon - ; - for?
   (a) to leave a comment, **(b) to keep things on the same line,** (c) to clear the screen, (d) to put in art

7. Which command let the user enter a choice?
   (a) enter, (b) put, **(c) input,** (d) choice, (e) option

8. What is the name of the program we are using?
   (a) QBasic, (b) Pascal, (c) C^{++}, **(d) ChipmunkBasic,** (e) Fortran

www.ingramcontent.com/pod-product-compliance
Lightning Source LLC
Chambersburg PA
CBHW080847170526
45158CB00009B/2655